# TRADING

## PSYCHOLOGY 2022

★ ★ ★

## DAY TRADING STRATEGIES FOR INVESTORS INVESTING SUCCESS

## SARA JACKLINE

# Trading Psychology 2022: Day Trading Strategies For Investors - Investing Success

# Trading psychology for investing success

In this article, we will look at our non-public strengths and the manner the ones form our improvement as members in economic markets. Years of operating with portfolio managers and buyers have taught me that the quality performers are not the ones with out weaknesses, however those who maximize specific cognitive and persona strengths. But what are our strengths, and the manner are we able to maximize them?

A specifically revolutionary technique to the evaluation of our capacities comes from the studies of Christopher Peterson and Martin Seligman. They advocate a framework of strengths it is a nice psychology counterpart to the great association of emotional disorders. This scheme defines 24 "man or woman strengths" that fall beneathneath six groupings of "virtues". The VIA Survey can be a standardized check that assesses those virtues and strengths, and it is to be had unfastened from charge, along a precis of our "signature strengths", "center strengths", and "lesser strengths". The virtues, as summarized via way of means of Lopez, Pedrotti, and Snyder of their reference quantity of nice psychology studies, include:

Wisdom and Knowledge - Cognitive strengths of collecting and making use of know-how;

Courage - Emotional strengths concerning self-control inside the pursuit of goals;

Humanity - Interpersonal strengths concerning worrying for others;

Justice - Community strengths concerning management and participation in groups;

Temperance - Behavioral strengths concerning strength of mind and perspective;

Transcendence - Spiritual strengths concerning connection to large reassets of meaning.

When cash managers searching for me out as a overall performance psychologist, they forever need to accurate or put off weaknesses. for instance, they might discover themselves unduly inspired via way of means of fear, greed, impatience, etc. and want to put off those feelings from their buying and selling. The strengths framework gives a unique technique to buying and selling psychology: Our best troubles in dealing with danger and uncertainty come from the suboptimal deployment of our strengths, now no longer always because of underlying weaknesses or emotional troubles that want remediation.

Consider the following standards that replicate my years of studies and commentary concerning overall performance in economic markets:

Distinctive fulfillment attracts upon specific strengths - Participants in markets who've loved lengthy and a hit careers are strangely robust in a single or greater of the man or woman strengths. for instance, one portfolio supervisor at a hedge fund has loved constant fulfillment for overflow a decade throughout very specific markets and marketplace conditions. His specific expertise/know-how strengths permit him to get precise thoughts for funding, and his specific temperance strengths have helped him manipulate positions with constant danger control and cautious maximization of praise relative to danger. Wherever we see the excellent overall performance we come across excellent electricity.

Poor overall performance in markets frequently follows from a failure to understand and make use of one's strengths - I've labored with buyers who've displayed specific interpersonal strengths, like the ones associated with the virtues of humanity and justice. after they can not channel those strengths into every day paintings processes— possibly via collaboration inside groups and consequently the cultivation of lively data networks—they emerge as frustrated, and consequently the disappointment hues their selection-making. for instance, one strangely social supervisor felt remoted and bored at the ground and attempted to compensate via way of means of buying and selling (over) actively to make stimulation. His hassle wasn't a scarcity of discipline, however the failure to domesticate a bit technique that tapped into his cappotential to persuade others and experience mutual give-and-take. Note additionally how our paintings environments (such due to the fact the configurations of conventional buying and selling flooring or the rigid shape of commercial enterprise meetings) can unwittingly frustrate the exercising of our strengths, ensuing in subpar overall performance.

Poor overall performance in markets frequently follows from overutilization of our signature strengths - a suited and beneficial evaluation of the "darkish side" of our persona trends comes from Hogan Assessments. The key concept is that, as soon as we emerge as rigidly grounded in signature strengths, the ones can convey undesirable effects. as an example, the dealer who pushes to increase danger-taking and gain better and higher profitability goals, taking the braveness distinctive feature to an extreme, can emerge as an underperformer whilst markets make radical shifts of their behavior, as took place in advance this year. Similarly, group leaders who're strangely supportive and level-headed inside the human distinctive feature can also additionally discover it tough to implement productiveness goals. pretty frequently this takes place whilst one signature electricity dominates to the cause that it interferes with the expression of different strengths.

The improvement of a hit buyers and traders hinges at the cultivation of "latent" strengths - this is mostly a simply vital idea and now no longer one it is well-appreciated. If overreliance on a electricity can convey undesirable effects and if simply shoring weaknesses will by no means create specific strengths, how are we to grow? the answer is located in what the VIA survey calls our "center strengths": capacities that we actually own however do not specifically discover with. These center strengths frequently are latent strengths if you want to be cultivated, bringing precise profits in overall performance. As I defined in the course of a current collection of weblog posts, an amazing way to figuring out those latent strengths is to own a person getting ready to us—a colleague, friend, or romantic partner—whole the strengths stock primarily based totally upon how they understand us. What we find out is that our closest contacts see strengths in us that we do not absolutely appreciate. These are frequently excellent applicants for latent strengths to develop. for instance, Mike Bellafiore and Seth Freudberg of SMB Capital lately defined a pinnacle dealer who took his overall performance to a alternative stage via way of means of workout creativity and range in how he expressed his thoughts. His danger-taking braveness changed into a extreme detail in his preliminary fulfillment, however it have been the latent strengths of expertise and temperance that allowed him to searching for out new approaches to seize praise relative to danger.

Successful types of buying and selling and funding are expressions of clusters of strengths - Unique overall performance displays intersections and integrations of strengths. as an example, one a hit portfolio supervisor I actually have labored with combines the virtues of data, humanity, justice, and transcendence to make a group tradition that emphasizes the growth of each one in every of its members, inspiring them to time and again domesticate and proportion new regions of experience. This cluster of strengths creates a dynamic group tradition that has been instrumental in recruiting pinnacle-great group members. Similarly, the combination of braveness and temperance can be a cluster not unusualplace to managers who gain excessive danger-adjusted returns. an amazing way to repose on our strengths is to discover how one electricity is frequently wont to specific another. If we want to emerge as less complicated in our justice virtues as a pacesetter, for instance, possibly we are able to channel the ones verbal exchange and teamwork capabilities via a transcendent experience of challenge and cause.

Too frequently I actually have visible that the effects of in depth paintings on weaknesses are an internalized experience of being weak. Day after day of focusing on our flaws unavoidably reinforces the experience of being flawed. The way to warding off this pitfall are to floor our overall performance critiques in our successes additionally as our shortcomings. as soon as we look at our successes, we find out signature and latent strengths in action, pointing the way to the answers quality geared up to gas our improvement. there aren't anyt any higher way to assessing our strengths—and clusters of strengths—than to observe how they show up themselves in our best overall performance. Our successes factor way to our greatness.

A few months ago, we imagined "thriving" as main our corporations to a miles higher everyday after the COVID-19 pandemic. Yet our duties as leaders now are in addition compounded via way of means of concurrent demanding situations of racial injustices, worldwide weather extrade, and financial uncertainties. going to "Thrive" seems greater onerous and lengthier than many oldsters imagined… or was hoping for.

The first wave and recurrences of COVID-19 nonetheless plague many components of the planet. Seventy-six percentage of agencies and plenty of geographies in our maximum up to date evaluation are nonetheless inside the Respond and Recover stages of the disaster[i]. Even agencies and geographies which have entered the Thrive segment understand that we beat this lengthy adventure collectively due to the fact our potentialities are inextricably linked.

The destiny of each one in every of our corporations, though, isn't always preordained. As resilient leaders, certainly considered one in every of our maximum critical roles right now is to preserve: to preserve our humans, a lot of whom are experiencing now no longer best fatigue however greater stresses than they ever have; to preserve our corporations in persevering with to make cost for all stakeholders, and to preserve society as it studies more than one existential threats. But while vital, we ought to additionally preserve our very own cappotential to persuade just so we are able to nonetheless serve over the lengthy adventure ahead.

Sustaining our humans

Our humans are present process unparalleled tiers of pressure and uncertainty: employees who've suffered deep non-public losses from COVID-19 and/or racial injustices; dad and mom stretching to navigate childcare and predominant uncertainties over training duties at the same time as nonetheless assembly paintings commitments; even the lack of simple grandchild-grandparent bodily connections. It calls for each empathy and braveness on our component to persuade them forward.

As leaders, we might want to empathize with and well known the myriad demanding situations our humans are presently dealing with, consisting of emotions of ambiguous loss and poisonous pressure.

With each ambiguous loss and poisonous pressure, the better definition of an endpoint and a reduction in uncertainty are vital approaches we are able to aid our groups. for instance, Deloitte has hosted Zoom-primarily based totally workshops in which a pass-segment of our humans helped to inform return-to-the place of job programs—giving them a more experience of control. Likewise, sponsoring tasks which have an mentioned endpoint and outcome—in which groups can claim that they're "done"—additionally enables to counter each ambiguous loss and poisonous pressure.

Additionally, having brave conversations is on the guts of taking decisive, formidable management actions, that are even greater essential now to maintaining our humans. Such conversations permit us to supply sincere messages and real-time comments amid the disaster, and want braveness:

To deal with tough conditions like commercial enterprise closures, layoffs, and furloughs as opposed to ignoring them and hoping they may be going away

to determine and enforce a direction of action, even if unpopular

To communicate the truth approximately things , why every selection changed into made, and well known the implications

Sustaining our corporations.


In the Respond segment of the disaster, maximum corporations' leaders located they had to play protection: preserving their values, their humans, their customers, and their commercial enterprise on the forefront. But to thrive inside the subsequent everyday, we will want to play each protection and offense, operating to shield our humans and our commercial enterprise, however additionally taking the longer view. we might want to lean into the wind and make contrarian movements now so we are able to start of the disaster with momentum and a aggressive edge. Many agencies will play protection, now no longer offense. Winners will do each[ii].

Crises normally spark off predominant possibilities like accelerating innovations, increasing environment relationships, looking forward to converting marketplace systems, and developing new commercial enterprise models. Many oldsters watched silos collapse nearly in a single day inside the rush to answer to COVID-19: Teams have become greater pass-functional, at the same time as thoughts, studies, resources, and knowledge have been speedy shared in approaches wherein enabled corporations to require greater informed, holistic actions. Leaders have to recollect which of those limitations are frequently completely removed.

# Sustaining society

Sustaining society calls for us as resilient leaders to require a very good greater lively function in influencing social structures and systems for the more proper. Leadership for the more proper calls for followership, and followership is engendered via way of means of the accept as true with.

Within society greater broadly, accept as true with is needed now greater urgently than ever, specifically amid the uncertainties of social disruption and consequently the converting function of establishments. As we recollect the organizational and institutional adjustments in structures and systems, constructing accept as true with goes to be important to effectively manual society.

Additionally, have an effect on is one of the essential impactful and lasting contributions. Where there may be racial or financial injustice, it is frequently ossified structures and entrenched establishments that perpetuate the unfair hooked up order. Given every of our corporations' big internet of relationships—with customers, vendors, environment partners, governments, communities—how are we able to join and leverage the whole cappotential of these networks to reform social structures and systems?

Sustaining our cappotential to persuade

We owe it to our humans, our corporations, and society to be individually slotted in mind, body, and cause to serve them over the stop of the day. Facing what can also be the most notable management venture in our lifetimes, the chance is that we are going to pass the depletion factor earlier than we understand it. We ought to now no longer best preserve others—we ought to preserve ourselves.

None oldsters capabilities lengthy the COVID-19 disaster will remaining or the path the virus will take. Likewise, the principle disruptions stemming from racial injustices, social inequality, worldwide weather extrade, and financial pressure can also additionally in addition extend the path to a "higher" everyday. As CEOs, we're referred to as upon to preserve via the disaster.

These maintaining duties are like a stone dropped in the course of a pond: The stone drops deep into the water, maintaining our cappotential to persuade via way of means of searching inward; the ripples attain bent preserve our personnel via way of means of on foot along them, our corporations via way of means of courageously refining the method and gambling offense, and society via way of means of making an investment in accept as true with to shape nice social extrade in establishments and structures.

# Best Stock Trading Courses for Learning at Home

Anyone with a few bucks and a web connection has the entirety they need to start off making an investment. But randomly choosing shares can be a recipe for failure. If you're extreme approximately making money, you would really like to first discover a way to take a position. For the ones attempting to find a place to start off, we've prepare this listing of the most effective inventory buying and selling guides out there.

Investing withinside the inventory change has in no way been easier… or cheaper. Once upon a time, traders wished to name up their private dealer to shape a alternate. The dealer could take a fee for their efforts, and voilà, transaction entire.

Then the net got here alongside and eliminated this pricey middleman. All you have to attempt to now could be energy up your pc and open an account. And a piece like that, the entirety of the inventory change is offered at your fingertips. But some of the ones fee prices controlled to live around… for a hint even as, at least.

Eventually, this democratization begat even extra get right of entry to. The budget-pleasant brokerage Robinhood brought fee-loose buying and selling in

2013. And rapidly after, complete-provider brokerages observed suit. lately, it's much less not unusualplace to rate a fee than not.

All of this short get right of entry to has captured the creativeness of could-be millionaires. Turning multiple penny shares into a touch fortune is each younger investor's dream. But the truth is, that's a fairly half-cocked approach… and a in particular not going route to monetary freedom.

There's an extensive distinction among hypothesis and making an investment. While speculators may search for high-praise trades, an knowledgeable investor is aware of the manner to reduce danger even as additionally maximizing profits. And those are some of the most effective inventory buying and selling guides we've determined to factor out you precisely the manner to do this.

The Five Best Stock Trading Courses (In No Particular Order)

Investing in Stocks: the whole Course ($139.99)

The Complete Foundation Stock Trading Course ($129.99)

University of Central Florida's Stocks, Bonds, and Investing: Oh, My! ($129.00)

Ultimate inventory change Investing: discover a way to Value Stocks ($49.99)

Options Trading: Candlestick Hacks for Options Trading ($109.99)

Investing in Stocks: the whole Course

Udemy is domestic to most of the guides on our listing. And completely reason. It gives a large library of open on line guides.

Some 35 million college students have enrolled in extra than four hundred million guides. And Steve Ballinger's

Investing in Stocks direction is that the No. 1 entire review of inventory making an investment withinside the location. Featuring eleven hours of on-call for video presentations, Ballinger's direction teaches new traders the bits and bobs of the inventory change.

By the end, visitors may have a corporation know-how of essential making an investment techniques. Using inventory screeners goes to be a habit. And Ballinger plies his college students with sufficient statistics to be equipped to decide danger ranges and the manner to apply qualitative and quantitative ratios to comply with nice practices. All of which makes this one the various most effective inventory buying and selling guides for logo spanking new traders.

## The Complete Foundation Stock Trading Course

This is some other direction designed for rookie investors. This one's different, though, due to the fact it's complete of theory, history, and strategy. This direction is proper for anyone who desires to surely apprehend how the inventory change works, additionally as its beginning and the manner it's developed over the years.

Once the foundation is laid, this direction informs new investors the manner to control danger. uncertain what number stocks to buy? that is frequently the proper direction for you. Professor Mohsen Hassan additionally spends an sincere quantity of it slow masking buying and selling psychology… a side of making an investment best too frequently omitted in lots of buying and selling guides.

By the pinnacle of this almost 10-hour direction, college students are going to be poised to take away feelings from a alternate – some thing that holds many traders returned from success. This factor of the direction – which even pro traders should use a refresher on – is what makes it one of the most effective inventory buying and selling guides available.

University of Central Florida's Stocks, Bonds, and Investing: Oh, My!

If you're capable of begin saving for retirement (and the sooner the better) however aren't certain in which to start off, that is frequently the direction for you. An alarming range of USA residents have however $5,000 earmarked for retirement. Even worse, 46% of oldsters don't even abilities plenty we've were given socked away.

This direction places college students at the the front strains in their future. It teaches them the manner to construct a different portfolio even as gaining familiarity with 401(k) and retirement plans. Students at some stage in this direction have the selection to decide an instructor-led model or a self-guided model. But what surely makes this one the various most effective inventory buying and selling guides is that it additionally covers private finance problems which are commonly omitted.

Ultimate inventory change Investing: discover a way to Value Stocks

If your concept beneficial making an investment is purchasing at Value City, boy, are we able to have a nice marvel for you. in best over 3 hours, college students of this direction will study the subtleties of one of the most a success making an investment techniques out there.

By the pinnacle of this direction, visitors will apprehend the basic concepts in the back of fee making an investment… and be equipped to identify undervalued and overestimated shares. Enrolled college students are also granted get right of entry to to a inventory valuation calculator that enables decide the really well worth of any inventory. there may be additionally a completely practical dialogue board for university youngsters to bop thoughts off the two professors.

Students will advantage the conceitedness to be equipped to pinpoint funding possibilities with peace of mind. that is frequently what makes this one the various most effective inventory buying and selling guides available in the marketplace today.

Options Trading: Candlestick Hacks for Options Trading

Looking to heighten your recreation and start turbocharging your portfolio? that is frequently the direction for you.

Getting began out in the global of buying and selling alternatives are frequently intimidating. But this direction absolutely demystifies the method.

If you're capable of take the bounce into technical evaluation and alternate correctly irrespective of the marketplace conditions, appearance no further. Over the direction of this five-hour class, the teachers element the manner to identify complicated styles and alternate correctly the use of them. interested by what "3 white soldiers" and "black crow" styles represent? How approximately "morning star" and "nighttime star" styles?

By the pinnacle of this direction, you won't even recall the Kenny Rogers tune of an equal name. But you'll ability to nicely make investments the use of the "nighttime star." And that's why that is frequently one of the most effective inventory buying and selling guides out there.

## School's Open. Are You capable of Learn?

The net has given us all short get right of entry to to the planet of making an investment. But some thing you're doing, don't begin tossing paychecks randomly shares. If you're capable of come to be a a success investor, it's vital to start off with an concept . And those are some of the most effective inventory buying and selling guides to help you're doing simply that.


But if you're beyond the reason of college and organized to start off making an investment directly , test in for the Trade of the Day e-letter. All you have to attempt to to is input your electronic mail cope with in the container to the proper… or down beneath if you're on a cellular device. You'll then obtain each day techniques to overcome the marketplace and offers your portfolio the wholesome enhance it needs.

# Our Strengths Shape Our Trading Psychology

In this article, we will look at our non-public strengths and the manner the ones form our improvement as members in economic markets. Years of operating with portfolio managers and buyers have taught me that the quality performers are not the ones with out weaknesses, however those who maximize specific cognitive and persona strengths. But what are our strengths, and the manner are we able to maximize them?

A specifically revolutionary technique to the evaluation of our capacities comes from the studies of Christopher Peterson and Martin Seligman. They advocate a framework of strengths it is a nice psychology counterpart to the great association of emotional disorders. This scheme defines 24 "man or woman strengths" that fall beneathneath six groupings of "virtues". The VIA Survey can be a standardized check that assesses those virtues and strengths, and it is to be had unfastened from charge, along a precis of our "signature strengths", "center strengths", and "lesser strengths". The virtues, as summarized via way of means of Lopez, Pedrotti, and Snyder of their reference quantity of nice psychology studies, include:

Wisdom and Knowledge - Cognitive strengths of collecting and making use of know-how;

Courage - Emotional strengths concerning self-control inside the pursuit of goals;

Humanity - Interpersonal strengths concerning worrying for others;

Justice - Community strengths concerning management and participation in groups;

Temperance - Behavioral strengths concerning strength of mind and perspective;

Transcendence - Spiritual strengths concerning connection to large reassets of meaning.

When cash managers searching for me out as a overall performance psychologist, they forever need to accurate or put off weaknesses. for instance, they might discover themselves unduly inspired via way of means of fear, greed, impatience, etc. and want to put off those feelings from their buying and selling. The strengths framework gives a unique technique to buying and selling psychology: Our best troubles in dealing with danger and uncertainty come from the suboptimal deployment of our strengths, now no longer always because of underlying weaknesses or emotional troubles that want remediation.

Consider the following standards that replicate my years of studies and commentary concerning overall performance in economic markets:

Distinctive fulfillment attracts upon specific strengths - Participants in markets who've loved lengthy and a hit careers are strangely robust in a single or greater of the man or woman strengths. for instance, one portfolio supervisor at a hedge fund has loved constant fulfillment for overflow a decade throughout very specific markets and marketplace conditions. His specific expertise/know-how strengths permit him to get precise thoughts for funding, and his specific temperance strengths have helped him manipulate positions with constant danger control and cautious maximization of praise relative to danger. Wherever we see the excellent overall performance we come across excellent electricity.

Poor overall performance in markets frequently follows from a failure to understand and make use of one's strengths - I've labored with buyers who've displayed specific interpersonal strengths, like the ones associated with the virtues of humanity and justice. after they can not channel those strengths into every day paintings processes— possibly via collaboration inside groups and consequently the cultivation of lively data networks—they emerge as frustrated, and consequently the disappointment hues their selection-making. for instance, one strangely social supervisor felt remoted and bored at the ground and attempted to compensate via way of means of buying and selling (over) actively to make stimulation. His hassle wasn't a scarcity of discipline, however the failure to domesticate a bit technique that tapped into his cappotential to persuade others and experience mutual give-and-take. Note additionally how our paintings environments (such due to the fact the configurations of conventional buying and selling flooring or the rigid shape of commercial enterprise meetings) can unwittingly frustrate the exercising of our strengths, ensuing in subpar overall performance.

Poor overall performance in markets frequently follows from overutilization of our signature strengths - a suited and beneficial evaluation of the "darkish side" of our persona trends comes from Hogan Assessments. The key concept is that, as soon as we emerge as rigidly grounded in signature strengths, the ones can convey undesirable effects. as an example, the dealer who pushes to increase danger-taking and gain better and higher profitability goals, taking the braveness distinctive feature to an extreme, can emerge as an underperformer whilst markets make radical shifts of their behavior, as took place in advance this year. Similarly, group leaders who're strangely supportive and level-headed inside the human distinctive feature can also additionally discover it tough to implement productiveness goals. pretty frequently this takes place whilst one signature electricity dominates to the cause that it interferes with the expression of different strengths.

The improvement of a hit buyers and traders hinges at the cultivation of "latent" strengths - this is mostly a simply vital idea and now no longer one it is well-appreciated. If overreliance on a electricity can convey undesirable effects and if simply shoring weaknesses will by no means create specific strengths, how are we to grow? the answer is located in what the VIA survey calls our "center strengths": capacities that we actually own however do not specifically discover with. These center strengths frequently are latent strengths if you want to be cultivated, bringing precise profits in overall performance. As I defined in the course of a current collection of weblog posts, an amazing way to figuring out those latent strengths is to own a person getting ready to us—a colleague, friend, or romantic partner—whole the strengths stock primarily based totally upon how they understand us. What we find out is that our closest contacts see strengths in us that we do not absolutely appreciate. These are frequently excellent applicants for latent strengths to develop. for instance, Mike Bellafiore and Seth Freudberg of SMB Capital lately defined a pinnacle dealer who took his overall performance to a alternative stage via way of means of workout creativity and range in how he expressed his thoughts. His danger-taking braveness changed into a extreme detail in his preliminary fulfillment, however it have been the latent strengths of expertise and temperance that allowed him to searching for out new approaches to seize praise relative to danger.

Successful types of buying and selling and funding are expressions of clusters of strengths - Unique overall performance displays intersections and integrations of strengths. as an example, one a hit portfolio supervisor I actually have labored with combines the virtues of data, humanity, justice, and transcendence to make a group tradition that emphasizes the growth of each one in every of its members, inspiring them to time and again domesticate and proportion new regions of experience. This cluster of strengths creates a dynamic group tradition that has been instrumental in recruiting pinnacle-great group members. Similarly, the combination of braveness and temperance can be a cluster not unusualplace to managers who gain excessive danger-adjusted returns. an amazing way to repose on our strengths is to discover how one electricity is frequently wont to specific another. If we want to emerge as less complicated in our justice virtues as a pacesetter, for instance, possibly we are able to channel the ones verbal exchange and teamwork capabilities via a transcendent experience of challenge and cause.

Too frequently I actually have visible that the effects of in depth paintings on weaknesses are an internalized experience of being weak. Day after day of focusing on our flaws unavoidably reinforces the experience of being flawed. The way to warding off this pitfall are to floor our overall performance critiques in our successes additionally as our shortcomings. as soon as we look at our successes, we find out signature and latent strengths in action, pointing the way to the answers quality geared up to gas our improvement. there aren't anyt any higher way to assessing our strengths—and clusters of strengths—than to observe how they show up themselves in our best overall performance. Our successes factor way to our greatness.

A few months ago, we imagined "thriving" as main our corporations to a miles higher everyday after the COVID-19 pandemic. Yet our duties as leaders now are in addition compounded via way of means of concurrent demanding situations of racial injustices, worldwide weather extrade, and financial uncertainties. going to "Thrive" seems greater onerous and lengthier than many oldsters imagined… or was hoping for.

The first wave and recurrences of COVID-19 nonetheless plague many components of the planet. Seventy-six percentage of agencies and plenty of geographies in our maximum up to date evaluation are nonetheless inside the Respond and Recover stages of the disaster[i]. Even agencies and geographies which have entered the Thrive segment understand that we beat this lengthy adventure collectively due to the fact our potentialities are inextricably linked.

The destiny of each one in every of our corporations, though, isn't always preordained. As resilient leaders, certainly considered one in every of our maximum critical roles right now is to preserve: to preserve our humans, a lot of whom are experiencing now no longer best fatigue however greater stresses than they ever have; to preserve our corporations in persevering with to make cost for all stakeholders, and to preserve society as it studies more than one existential threats. But while vital, we ought to additionally preserve our very own cappotential to persuade just so we are able to nonetheless serve over the lengthy adventure ahead.

Sustaining our humans

Our humans are present process unparalleled tiers of pressure and uncertainty: employees who've suffered deep non-public losses from COVID-19 and/or racial injustices; dad and mom stretching to navigate childcare and predominant uncertainties over training duties at the same time as nonetheless assembly paintings commitments; even the lack of simple grandchild-grandparent bodily connections. It calls for each empathy and braveness on our component to persuade them forward.

As leaders, we might want to empathize with and well known the myriad demanding situations our humans are presently dealing with, consisting of emotions of ambiguous loss and poisonous pressure.

With each ambiguous loss and poisonous pressure, the better definition of an endpoint and a reduction in uncertainty are vital approaches we are able to aid our groups. for instance, Deloitte has hosted Zoom-primarily based totally workshops in which a pass-segment of our humans helped to inform return-to-the place of job programs—giving them a more experience of control. Likewise, sponsoring tasks which have an mentioned endpoint and outcome—in which groups can claim that they're "done"—additionally enables to counter each ambiguous loss and poisonous pressure.

Additionally, having brave conversations is on the guts of taking decisive, formidable management actions, that are even greater essential now to maintaining our humans. Such conversations permit us to supply sincere messages and real-time comments amid the disaster, and want braveness:

To deal with tough conditions like commercial enterprise closures, layoffs, and furloughs as opposed to ignoring them and hoping they may be going away

to determine and enforce a direction of action, even if unpopular

To communicate the truth approximately things , why every selection changed into made, and well known the implications

Sustaining our corporations.


In the Respond segment of the disaster, maximum corporations' leaders located they had to play protection: preserving their values, their humans, their customers, and their commercial enterprise on the forefront. But to thrive inside the subsequent everyday, we will want to play each protection and offense, operating to shield our humans and our commercial enterprise, however additionally taking the longer view. we might want to lean into the wind and make contrarian movements now so we are able to start of the disaster with momentum and a aggressive edge. Many agencies will play protection, now no longer offense. Winners will do each[ii].

Crises normally spark off predominant possibilities like accelerating innovations, increasing environment relationships, looking forward to converting marketplace systems, and developing new commercial enterprise models. Many oldsters watched silos collapse nearly in a single day inside the rush to answer to COVID-19: Teams have become greater pass-functional, at the same time as thoughts, studies, resources, and knowledge have been speedy shared in approaches wherein enabled corporations to require greater informed, holistic actions. Leaders have to recollect which of those limitations are frequently completely removed.

# Sustaining society

Sustaining society calls for us as resilient leaders to require a very good greater lively function in influencing social structures and systems for the more proper. Leadership for the more proper calls for followership, and followership is engendered via way of means of the accept as true with.

Within society greater broadly, accept as true with is needed now greater urgently than ever, specifically amid the uncertainties of social disruption and consequently the converting function of establishments. As we recollect the organizational and institutional adjustments in structures and systems, constructing accept as true with goes to be important to effectively manual society.

Additionally, have an effect on is one of the essential impactful and lasting contributions. Where there may be racial or financial injustice, it is frequently ossified structures and entrenched establishments that perpetuate the unfair hooked up order. Given every of our corporations' big internet of relationships—with customers, vendors, environment partners, governments, communities—how are we able to join and leverage the whole cappotential of these networks to reform social structures and systems?

Sustaining our cappotential to persuade

We owe it to our humans, our corporations, and society to be individually slotted in mind, body, and cause to serve them over the stop of the day. Facing what can also be the most notable management venture in our lifetimes, the chance is that we are going to pass the depletion factor earlier than we understand it. We ought to now no longer best preserve others—we ought to preserve ourselves.

None oldsters capabilities lengthy the COVID-19 disaster will remaining or the path the virus will take. Likewise, the principle disruptions stemming from racial injustices, social inequality, worldwide weather extrade, and financial pressure can also additionally in addition extend the path to a "higher" everyday. As CEOs, we're referred to as upon to preserve via the disaster.

These maintaining duties are like a stone dropped in the course of a pond: The stone drops deep into the water, maintaining our cappotential to persuade via way of means of searching inward; the ripples attain bent preserve our personnel via way of means of on foot along them, our corporations via way of means of courageously refining the method and gambling offense, and society via way of means of making an investment in accept as true with to shape nice social extrade in establishments and structures.

# Day Trading Strategies for Investors

The excellent day buying and selling techniques evolve every and every year. New types of analysis, sample identification, and some distance greater can affect traders. And as you will know, day buyers are a unique breed altogether. constant with a present day Trader report, there are pretty thirteen million day buyers worldwide.

four freshest Day Trading Strategies

Day buyers apprehend that there are a couple of methods to reach and hold triumphing positions at some stage in each day. From trailing stops to income targets, you will pre-decide when you get out.

But no two-day buyers suppose precisely alike. In fact, maximum of these traders have their personal set of guidelines, concepts, or even quirky superstitions. Whatever works to induce ahead, they are going to apply it. and that they may preserve the use of it till their success runs out.

Yet there are 4 famous day buying and selling techniques which might be most typical in today's inventory marketplace:

Daily Pivoting

Fading

Movement Trading

Scalping.

Each of those techniques makes use of distinct techniques. But finding out while to promote perhaps a uniform idea. Day buying and selling can be a full-time job, and maximum buyers will outline precisely as soon as they may promote earlier than shopping for a inventory withinside the first place. Let's take a higher take a look at out those 4-day buying and selling techniques below.

# Daily Pivoting

Stock volatility is the call of the game while it includes day by day pivot buying and selling. and consequently the aim is to buy the inventory at its lowest rate each day and promote at its maximum rate.

These are called the "pivot factors" that traders use as indicators. Specifically, they use proportion rate highs, lows, and previous day final costs to calculate pivot factors for the existing day. This has come to be one of the principal not unusualplace day buying and selling techniques for figuring out marketplace developments over distinct intervals of your time.

## Fading

Fading is all approximately shorting shares. And quick sale can be a buying and selling idea at some stage in that you speculate at the decline of a inventory rate.

You start via way of means of borrowing stocks of a inventory which you certainly trust will lower in value. Next, you promote those borrowed stocks to shoppers who're inclined to pay the marketplace value.

Theoretically, you are having a bet that the percentage rate will nevertheless decline earlier than the borrowed stocks ought to be returned.

You are relying on and taking benefit of the drop withinside the inventory rate. However, this is usually a manner greater superior type of buying and selling it is now no longer encouraged for day buying and selling beginners.

Movement Trading

Did you understand that information reviews and economic updates can play a challenge at some stage in a inventory's increase or decline? Well, motion buyers simply do.

The motion approach is made round spotting developments and gambling off information releases. Day buyers purchase a inventory that has excessive extent guide and rides it out till there are symptoms and symptoms of the fashion reversing. At that time, they promote their stocks, with a bit of luck for a income. It's as easy as that.

## Scalping

Scalping is one of the principal famous day buying and selling techniques you will find. that is frequently as it gets rid of the most quantity of threat as feasible at some stage in a excessive-threat marketplace. Day buyers fight the most quantity of threat as anyone. But scalping facilitates decrease that threat via way of means of buying and selling shares as quickly as positions come to be profitable.

Scalpers aren't inclined to require possibilities and watch for large returns. the immediate a inventory rate turns into advantageous, the dealer will promote for a bit income. By doing this again and again at some stage in the day, those buyers can increase hefty gains.

However, scalping additionally calls for you to promote a inventory as quickly as it starts to drop additionally. That manner, you are taking on a bit loss and develop earlier than the inventory falls any longer.

Best Day Trading Strategies for You

As you presently know, there are numerous methods to journey approximately day buying and selling. Yet that is frequently some distance greater than a hobby. Your willpower will want to move nicely past your buying and selling time. It takes prolonged studies and non-stop oversight to come to be every day dealer.

# Day Trading Rules for New Stock Traders

In this article, we're going to observe our non-public strengths and the manner the ones form our improvement as members in monetary markets. Years of operating with portfolio managers and investors have taught me that the excellent performers are not the ones with out weaknesses, however people who maximize exceptional cognitive and persona strengths. But what are our strengths, and the manner are we able to maximize them?

A especially progressive method to the evaluation of our capacities comes from the studies of Christopher Peterson and Martin Seligman. They recommend a framework of strengths that is a tremendous psychology counterpart to the great association of emotional disorders. This scheme defines 24 "person strengths" that fall beneathneath six groupings of "virtues". The VIA Survey can be a standardized check that assesses those virtues and strengths, and it is to be had loose from charge, along a precis of our "signature strengths", "center strengths", and "lesser strengths". The virtues, as summarized with the aid of using Lopez, Pedrotti, and Snyder of their reference quantity of tremendous psychology studies, include:

Wisdom and Knowledge - Cognitive strengths of accumulating and making use of understanding;

Courage - Emotional strengths regarding self-discipline in the pursuit of goals;

Humanity - Interpersonal strengths regarding being concerned for others;

Justice - Community strengths regarding management and participation in groups;

Temperance - Behavioral strengths regarding strength of mind and perspective;

Transcendence - Spiritual strengths regarding connection to large reassets of meaning.

When cash managers are looking for me out as a overall performance psychologist, they always need to accurate or do away with weaknesses. for instance, they may locate themselves unduly stimulated with the aid of using fear, greed, impatience, etc. and want to do away with those feelings from their buying and selling. The strengths framework gives a unique method to buying and selling psychology: Our finest troubles in dealing with chance and uncertainty come from the suboptimal deployment of our strengths, now no longer always because of underlying weaknesses or emotional troubles that want remediation.

Consider the following concepts that replicate my years of studies and remark concerning overall performance in monetary markets:

Distinctive achievement attracts upon exceptional strengths - Participants in markets who've loved lengthy and a hit careers are strangely sturdy in a single or greater of the person strengths. for instance, one portfolio supervisor at a hedge fund has loved regular achievement for overflow a decade throughout very exclusive markets and marketplace conditions. His exceptional information/understanding strengths allow him to get specific thoughts for funding, and his exceptional temperance strengths have helped him control positions with regular chance control and cautious maximization of praise relative to chance. Wherever we see the brilliant overall performance we come upon brilliant electricity.

Poor overall performance in markets frequently follows from a failure to understand and make use of one's strengths - I've labored with investors who've displayed unique interpersonal strengths, like the ones associated with the virtues of humanity and justice. after they can not channel those strengths into each day paintings processes— possibly via collaboration inside groups and consequently the cultivation of lively records networks—they come to be frustrated, and consequently the disappointment shades their choice-making. for instance, one strangely social supervisor felt remoted and bored at the ground and attempted to compensate with the aid of using buying and selling (over) actively to make stimulation. His trouble wasn't a scarcity of discipline, however the failure to domesticate a chunk system that tapped into his cappotential to persuade others and revel in mutual give-and-take. Note additionally how our paintings environments (such due to the fact the configurations of conventional buying and selling flooring or the rigid shape of commercial enterprise meetings) can unwittingly frustrate the workout of our strengths, ensuing in subpar overall performance.

Poor overall performance in markets frequently follows from overutilization of our signature strengths - a suitable and beneficial evaluation of the "darkish side" of our persona trends comes from Hogan Assessments. The key concept is that, as soon as we come to be rigidly grounded in signature strengths, the ones can deliver undesirable results. as an example, the dealer who pushes to increase chance-taking and attain better and higher profitability goals, taking the braveness distinctive feature to an extreme, can come to be an underperformer whilst markets make radical shifts of their behavior, as took place in advance this year. Similarly, crew leaders who're strangely supportive and level-headed in the human distinctive feature might also additionally locate it tough to implement productiveness goals. pretty frequently this takes place whilst one signature electricity dominates to the motive that it interferes with the expression of different strengths.

The improvement of a hit investors and traders hinges at the cultivation of "latent" strengths - this is usually a clearly essential idea and now no longer one that is well-appreciated. If overreliance on a electricity can deliver undesirable results and if simply shoring weaknesses will by no means create exceptional strengths, how are we to grow? the answer is observed in what the VIA survey calls our "center strengths": capacities that we simply own however do not especially perceive with. These center strengths frequently are latent strengths with a purpose to be cultivated, bringing specific profits in overall performance. As I defined in the course of a latest collection of weblog posts, an splendid way to figuring out those latent strengths is to own a person on the point of us—a colleague, friend, or romantic partner—entire the strengths stock primarily based totally upon how they understand us. What we find out is that our closest contacts see strengths in us that we do not completely appreciate. These are frequently brilliant applicants for latent strengths to develop. for instance, Mike Bellafiore and Seth Freudberg of SMB Capital currently defined a pinnacle dealer who took his overall performance to a alternative stage with the aid of using workout creativity and range in how he expressed his thoughts. His chance-taking braveness turned into a critical detail in his preliminary achievement, however it were the latent strengths of information and temperance that allowed him to are looking for out new methods to seize praise relative to chance.

Successful kinds of buying and selling and funding are expressions of clusters of strengths - Unique overall performance displays intersections and integrations of strengths. as an example, one a hit portfolio supervisor I actually have labored with combines the virtues of data, humanity, justice, and transcendence to make a crew way of life that emphasizes the growth of each one in every of its members, inspiring them to again and again domesticate and proportion new regions of experience. This cluster of strengths creates a dynamic crew way of life that has been instrumental in recruiting pinnacle-great crew members. Similarly, the combination of braveness and temperance can be a cluster not unusualplace to managers who attain excessive chance-adjusted returns. an splendid way to repose on our strengths is to discover how one electricity is frequently wont to specific another. If we desire to come to be less difficult in our justice virtues as a pacesetter, for instance, possibly we can channel the ones communique and teamwork competencies via a transcendent feel of task and motive.

Too frequently I actually have visible that the effects of in depth paintings on weaknesses are an internalized feel of being weak. Day after day of focusing on our flaws unavoidably reinforces the feel of being flawed. The way to warding off this pitfall are to floor our overall performance critiques in our successes additionally as our shortcomings. as soon as we observe our successes, we find out signature and latent strengths in action, pointing the way to the answers excellent geared up to gas our improvement. there aren't anyt any higher way to assessing our strengths—and clusters of strengths—than to observe how they occur themselves in our finest overall performance. Our successes factor way to our greatness.

## Leadership

A few months ago, we imagined "thriving" as main our companies to a miles higher ordinary after the COVID-19 pandemic. Yet our duties as leaders now are similarly compounded with the aid of using concurrent demanding situations of racial injustices, worldwide weather change, and financial uncertainties. going to "Thrive" seems greater laborious and lengthier than many oldsters imagined… or was hoping for.

The first wave and recurrences of COVID-19 nevertheless plague many elements of the planet. Seventy-six percentage of agencies and plenty of geographies in our maximum updated evaluation are nevertheless in the Respond and Recover levels of the crisis[i]. Even agencies and geographies which have entered the Thrive section comprehend that we beat this lengthy adventure collectively due to the fact our possibilities are inextricably linked.

The destiny of each one in every of our companies, though, is not preordained. As resilient leaders, certainly considered one in every of our maximum important roles at once is to maintain: to maintain our humans, a lot of whom are experiencing now no longer most effective fatigue however greater stresses than they ever have; to maintain our companies in persevering with to make fee for all stakeholders, and to maintain society as it reviews more than one existential threats. But whilst essential, we ought to additionally maintain our very own cappotential to persuade simply so we can nevertheless serve over the lengthy adventure ahead.

## Sustaining our humans

Our humans are present process unheard of degrees of pressure and uncertainty: employees who've suffered deep non-public losses from COVID-19 and/or racial injustices; mother and father stretching to navigate childcare and foremost uncertainties over education duties even as nevertheless assembly paintings commitments; even the lack of fundamental grandchild-grandparent bodily connections. It calls for each empathy and braveness on our component to persuade them forward.

As leaders, we might want to empathize with and well known the myriad demanding situations our humans are presently dealing with, along with emotions of ambiguous loss and poisonous pressure.

With each ambiguous loss and poisonous pressure, the better definition of an endpoint and a reduction in uncertainty are essential methods we can guide our groups. for instance, Deloitte has hosted Zoom-primarily based totally workshops in which a cross-phase of our humans helped to inform return-to-the place of work programs—giving them a more feel of control. Likewise, sponsoring tasks which have an mentioned endpoint and outcome—in which groups can claim that they're "done"—additionally facilitates to counter each ambiguous loss and poisonous pressure.

Additionally, having brave conversations is on the guts of taking decisive, ambitious management actions, that are even greater important now to maintaining our humans. Such conversations allow us to supply straightforward messages and real-time remarks amid the crisis, and want braveness:

To cope with tough conditions like commercial enterprise closures, layoffs, and furloughs as opposed to ignoring them and hoping they're going away

to choose and put in force a path of action, even if unpopular

To talk the truth approximately things , why every choice turned into made, and well known the implications

Sustaining our companies

# SARA JACKLINE

www.ingramcontent.com/pod-product-compliance
Lightning Source LLC
Chambersburg PA
CBHW081945160726
47999CB00008B/2519